MOVE THE
CROWD

MOVE THE

CROWD

Voices and Faces of the Hip-Hop Nation

Gregor and Dimitri Ehrlich

Photographs by Jesse Frohman

Pocket Books

MTV books

New York London Toronto
Sydney Tokyo Singapore

For our father, Milton Paul Ehrlich, who suggested that we write this book.

Vast waves of gratitude to the immensely talented and extraordinary Jesse Frohman, who contributed all of the photographs in this book.

Deep thanks to Ginny Brown, who typed up the original manuscript version of this text, to Bill and Jane Appleton, who were kind enough to loan us their trusty Mac, to Theo Newman, who gathered tremendous amounts of research, and to Ken Dreifach, who put his job on the line for us without even knowing it.

Special shout-outs to Eduardo Braniff at MTV Books for embracing this idea, to our agent Andrew Blauner and to extra clever Pocket Books editor Paul Schnee and his supreme editorial assistant Calaya Reid for helping to make it a reality.

Big respect to old school hip-hop expert Greg Graf, for furious styles and various skills.

Love to Alexis, Bruce, Max, and Oliver Menken, and to Etta B. Ehrlich who *is* hip-hop.

If it hadn't been for Greg Brown, who was a great dancer and a great friend and who was into rap before anybody we knew, our lives would have been much duller and this book would not exist. We miss him every day.

Some portions of this material have appeared previously in the following publications: *The New York Times, Vibe, Details, The London Observer, Manhattan File, Interview, Tower Records Pulse, Spin, Rap Pages, Spice, Hits Magazine, Downtown Express, Entertainment Weekly, L.A. Style, Madamoiselle, The Guardian, New York Newsday, Huh!, Speak, N.Y.Q.,* and *Rolling Stone.*

An Original Publication of
MTV BOOKS/POCKET BOOKS

POCKET BOOKS, a division of Simon & Schuster, Inc.
1230 Avenue of the Americas, New York, NY 10020

COVER PHOTOGRAPHS BY JESSE FROHMAN

COVER AND INTERIOR DESIGN BY JOEL AVIROM AND JASON SNYDER

Printed in Canada

CONTENTS

"Rap **dictates** and it **reflects.** You better **know your history** before you start talking off the cuff."

—Chuck D

In 1979, when "Rapper's Delight" came out, crashing rap's first wave into the national consciousness, a friend brought the record over, the shiny light-blue sleeve of the twelve-inch like a slice of sky, portending the boundless future of hip-hop. But nobody knew that at the time. We memorized the "bang-bang-da-boogie-da-up-jump-da-boogie-and-it's-up-jump-boogie-da-beat" lyrics and our friend, more ahead of the curve than we (or most of our white suburban New Jersey friends) were, coaxed us into buying Adidas track suits, Pumas with fat laces, and Gazelle glasses, and did his best to teach us the few break-dancing moves he had learned. We couldn't break to save our lives but that didn't stop us from getting on a bus to New York City to bust our three or four hard-earned moves in Washington Square Park. Having spent the last few months popping and snapping alongside him, it was showtime. He had actually managed to do the worm, in which he would drop straight to the floor and undulate like an eel, and was so good that we got caught up in his enthusiasm and learned a lesson: it's not where you're from, it's where your heart is.

That day in the park, real break-dancers from Brooklyn showed up, and made the asphalt look as soft and pliable as black rubber. They bounced their skinny chests against it. They spun on the tops of their heads while holding cigarettes in their mouths. It was breathtaking, like kung-fu and rock 'n' roll rolled into one. We didn't know what had hit us. But we knew better than to bust out our measly maneuvers in the presence of the real thing, and went home full of awe.

While our careers as break-dancers were mercifully brief, our love affair with rap was just getting started. Over the next few years, we memorized all the words to songs like, "The Breaks" by Kurtis Blow and "The Message" by Grandmaster Flash, scrutinizing them with Talmudic scholarliness. We appropriated hip-hop almost as lustfully as it appropriated pop culture.

But when the day came in June 1986 that we heard Boogie Down Productions' first album, *Criminal Minded*, it was obvious something had changed. It was on a cassette made by that same friend who had brought "Rapper's Delight" into our lives, and it had Eric B. and Rakim's "Paid in Full" on the other side. Hip-hop had grown immensely since 1979 of course, but this was a long way from "Rapper's Delight." Loaded with aggression, humor, and bristling with confidence, *Criminal Minded* was a sonic satori. The old order had been overturned by Rakim and KRS-One.

A few weeks later, we were sitting in a car in Washington Heights, listening to "South Bronx," a single from *Criminal Minded*. "South Bronx" is a tribal chant of pride in the borough were hip-hop was born, and includes one of rap's most territorial battle cries: "So you think that hip-hop got its start out in Queensbridge? Pop that junk up in the Bronx and you might not live." Hearing that stomping, raw, invincible sound, our palms hitting the steering wheel in time to the elemental beat, we knew then that rock music hadn't just been outdone. It had been replaced. While it took a few years for the truth of that revelation to hit the malls, the momentum of hip-hop still hasn't died out.

It really doesn't matter exactly when rap started. It was a tsunami and it drenched America. As with "Rapper's Delight," sometimes tsunamis seem like mild-mannered whitecaps when they're gathering strength a mile out from shore, but when they hit, your life is changed and turned upside down forever. Sitting in that car in Washington Heights, we talked about how great it would be to have a job where you listened to hip-hop all day. It dawned on us with total clarity that hip-hop was the bomb we had been waiting for, the crowbar every generation needs to pry themselves free of their parents. And it did not let us down.

We're not going to use the following pages to rehash that same old story about how hip-hop began in the Bronx in the early 1970s, when a Jamaican-born DJ named Kool Herc began cutting and scratching on a turntable. This book is about how hip-hop feels, the music itself: its own truth, its circuitous anti-logic. Its atonal jackhammer entry into our subconscious. Its energy, humor, and directness, and its subversive, creative intelligence, manifested most beautifully in the way hip-hop appropriated mainstream culture and music. It was, for a while at least, the most unselfconsciously defiant art form.

Understanding the power of hip-hop isn't something you can get from an encyclopedic history. It is understood driving through New York City, trapped in white-light August heat and traffic, the music serving as a psychic valve, a vest and roof-mounted gun, spraying anger, making the traffic, heat, and gasoline fumes into one perfect entity. It is music that can make it fun to be stuck in a traffic jam.

Hip-hop is understood walking to work through midtown Manhattan, listening to the playback of a college radio show taped the night before, hearing N.W.A's "Fuck Tha Police" for the first time, ripping through our flimsy Walkman headphones.

The power of hip-hop is understood in an airport in Miami in May 1990, absentmindedly loading an advance cassette of Ice Cube's "AmeriKKKa's Most Wanted" into the Walkman, expecting nothing in particular. Suddenly: *WHAM*. It was like a pit bull loaded on malt liquor, tearing into your ears, and it felt good. We were ecstatic and had to rewind the thing over and over, incredulous at the pure adrenaline rush. We wished we could have dialed up a hip-hop broker on Wall Street and bought stock in Ice Cube then, a few months before the album exploded and sold millions.

But hip-hop is more than just the music. It is the people who make it. It is a day spent driving around in Hempstead, Long Island, with Flavor Flav, careening through red lights, not sure whether to be scared because of his driving or just to strive to remember every detail to tell our friends. The engine of his puke-green Corvette rocketed us to some awful fast-food restaurant where we observed that yes, he did have to take out his famous gold fronts before eating.

A lot of the best moments in personal hip-hop history weren't recorded, like the evening spent hanging out with Q-Tip, sipping terrible champagne, talking about girls (until his girlfriend showed up). Or the night Pete Nice swung by our apartment in his BMW and drove us around Manhattan excitedly cranking rough mixes of the new 3rd Bass album, and the cops pulled the car over. Or finding Hank Shocklee asleep on the couch at Green Street recording studios, watching him wake up and go back to the new beats he was creating for Public Enemy.

Neither did we have a tape recorder handy the first time we ran into KRS-One on 34th Street and 3rd Avenue; he was bemused by us asking for his autograph, and his manager's number too so we could set up an interview. That was near the apartment where he lived with Ms. Melody for a while, where we once went to pick him up, to drive down to Chinatown for a vegetarian dinner to interview him for *Spin* magazine, and our mom came along.

Our question as we sat down to write this book was: How to get at the essence of what hip-hop was like in those innocent years, how to immerse the reader in what it felt like? The interviews that form the basis for the quotes in this book span ten years, and the scene has changed considerably. Hip-hop evolves according to an accelerated clock, one whose arms swing even faster than the timepiece of pop culture in general.

One thing that hasn't changed is the way rap is still misunderstood by those who choose not to listen to it. Perhaps the most widely held misperception about hip-hop is that it is somehow one thing. Rap, like the broader black culture from which it developed, is far from monolithic. The sociologist Claude Lévi-Strauss said that all cultures are processes; they are constantly changing ways of assigning meaning to things in our lives. So the best way to understand a culture is to hear what it means from the people—in this case the rappers—themselves. We went back to our interviews to discern the essence of what they were talking about.

In the two decades that have passed since "Rapper's Delight" blew up, hip-hop has permeated, and in many ways co-opted, popular culture. The term now includes not only the three original elements that gave hip-hop culture its sonic, visual, and physical form—music, graffiti, and break-dancing—but also television, film, fashion, and publishing. The word has gone from referring to an inner-city culture to conveying a certain aesthetic, so that a "hip-hop sensibility" can now reasonably be applied to virtually anything—a stand-up comedian, a talk show, a cookbook, a comic strip, or a line of greeting cards. And of course, the music's place in pop culture just keeps getting bigger: from 1995 to 1998 rap became the fastest-growing genre, with sales growth of 51% during that three-year period. With 62 million albums sold in 1997, rap is now poised to surpass sales of country music, which is currently the best-selling genre.

Fifty years ago, Ralph Ellison asserted that all of what is considered uniquely American culture is Afro-American. But there's an irony to the cultural ascendancy of hip-hop in America, since rap is fundamentally the voice of a marginalized segment of society; while hip-hop is concerned with many things—from humor to sex to money—a considerable portion of hip-hop has been devoted to decrying the way America's racist power structure debases Afro-American life. As with reggae in the early 1970s, in the 1980s rap's overt anger and righteous indignation was quickly embraced by white youth culture at least partly because we needed something with which to individuate ourselves from our boomer parents. If your mom grew up on Bob Dylan and your hormones are urging you into adolescent rebellion, cranking Tom

Petty isn't quite going to shock her. Master P., with his gold-plated tank rolling onto a basketball court, has a little more voltage.

Of course, rap's crossover into mainstream—read: white—America is only part of the music's trajectory over the last twenty years. While hip-hop is still only one among many elements in the broader black culture, it has developed into a juggernaut—both economically and aesthetically—that now occupies a singular place on the black American landscape.

That fact, too, is not without a certain irony. As sociologist Orlando Patterson argues in *The Ordeal of Integration: Progress and Resentment in America's Racial Crisis*: "The paradox is this: for the great majority of Afro-Americans, these are genuinely the best of times, but for a minority they would seem to be, relatively, among the worst, at least since the ending of formal Jim Crow laws." Having been enslaved, kept in semi-serfdom, violently segregated, wantonly oppressed, and discriminated against, black Americans are now better off than at any time in their history. As Patterson says, "Viewed from the perspective of comparative history and sociology, it can be said, unconditionally, that the changes that have taken place in the United States over the last fifty years are unparalleled in the history of majority-minority relations." One thing is certain: it's impossible to consider and understand hip-hop outside the context of race; the music remains so inextricably linked with black culture that it is nearly impossible to separate them.

Being white and writing about rap is, in itself, something of an issue. As outsiders who spent some time on the inside, how could we legitimately represent the essence of a specifically black musical idiom?

Grappling with this question, we figured rather than writing the story ourselves, we would listen to the people who made it happen, and write down what we heard. What follows is a series of quotes-as-snapshots, taken over the course of the decade and told in the words of the rappers themselves.

13

The mid-1980s through the early 1990s was a period during which rap entered what might be called its "golden age," not because those were the best years but because they were the defining years. There aren't any hard dates we're pointing to as a creative high point, but like jazz during the heyday of bebop and rock at the height of psychedelia, hip-hop went through a period of self-definition and quantum creative leaps. It is more commonly accepted that rap's golden era was during the "old school" era—that innocent time when "Rapper's Delight" first brought hip-hop to the masses. One of the underlying premises of this book is that rap's defining years were loosely sandwiched between the end of the old school era and the rise of gangsta rap. At the time, of course, the music was called "new school," a period that began with the release of Eric B. and Rakim's 1986 single "Eric B. Is President." Other milestone records include Slick Rick's *The Great Adventures of Slick Rick*, Boogie Down Productions' *Criminal Minded*, Public Enemy's first and second albums, and debuts by Biz Markie, Audio II, MC Lyte, Rob Base, and Big Daddy Kane. By today's standards, these were mainly simple, cheaply made recordings: an elemental beat and some unselfconscious—often hilarious—rhymes thrown down quickly. This was a time when rappers still wrote and recorded with a liberating unawareness of the presence of a potentially huge international audience. Singles like Biz Markie's "Picking Boogers" and Audio II's "Top Billin" had playful qualities that have become more noticeable by their conspicuous absence from today's hip-hop. No matter how much more recording technology "advanced," somehow later artists were never really able to outdo the raw perfection of records like B.D.P.'s "South Bronx." As with some great three-chord rock 'n' roll songs, there remains a sense of being right on the spot, an almost Zen kind of immediacy to these singles that no amount of money, polish, or effort can duplicate.

By the late 1980s, rap had fragmented in two directions: abstract and gangsta. The energy and optimism spilled into the Native Tongues movement, a trend toward Afrocentrism, in which a gentler, abstract, less syncopated rhyme flow ruled, accompanied by eclectic sampling and a greater musicality. Thick gold chains were supplanted by thick wooden beads, while A Tribe Called Quest, the Jungle Brothers, and De La Soul explored hip-hop's boundaries, evincing a sense that rap could go anywhere and do anything.

Then, from another end of the continent, came N.W.A's *Straight Outta Compton*, an album that dropped like a guillotine blade. Nihilistically defiant, it started a bicoastal lyrical arms race that really hasn't abated. Unequivocal in a way not heard of since the heyday of punk rock more than a decade earlier, Niggaz With Attitude almost singlehandedly brought an end to the period of New York's musical hegemony. N.W.A. also proved it was possible to sell a million copies of a record with absolutely no radio play. *Straight Outta Compton* was the album that pushed hip-hop into suburban America. It was something so forceful and disturbing to most parents that it really couldn't have failed to get inside the bedrooms of adolescent male white America. The single that earned the album its initial notoriety with the F.B.I. was "Fuck Tha Police," a track that also featured the national debuts of two voices that would become major players in 1990s hip-hop: Ice Cube and Dr. Dre.

Since then, there have been a series of other plateaus in rap's development, but they have been more evolutionary than revolutionary. These include the rise of Dr. Dre and Snoop Doggy Dogg, the Geto Boys, Tupac, the Wu-Tang Clan, and many others. From an artistic point of view, the release of Biggie Smalls' debut, *Ready to Die*, might be the apex of all these years of hip-hop's creative escalation—it's hard to imagine any raps better than the rhymes Smalls conjured on the first six tracks of that album. Regardless, this book is not intended to catalog rap's greatest moments or to be an encyclopedia; it's a celebration. We don't aim to be comprehensive, we aim to plunge readers into a world, to immerse them in what hip-hop tastes like.

Having conducted several hundred interviews with rappers during the course of the last decade for magazines ranging from the early rap fanzines (*Spice, Rap Pages, Word Up,* and so on) as well as mainstream publications like *Rolling Stone, Spin, Details, Interview,* and *The New York Times,* we culled through the transcripts in search of those comments from rappers that leapt out at us with the most "self-selecting vividness" to borrow a phrase from Allen Ginsberg. We think it matters that every one of the quotes in this book came from interviews we conducted, that we met and spoke with all of the rappers in this book, if only because different interviewers would have asked different questions and gotten different answers. In compiling this text we eliminated our questions to put the spotlight on the way the emcees spoke. Hip-hop came directly from the mouths of the people you will meet in the following pages. Visceral, onomatopoeic, and loaded with the kind of juice most poets dream about tapping into, the best rap feels spontaneous and competitive, like a surprise knockout. Like the angular, electrifying language that gives the best rap its dynamism and odd grace, these quotes were chosen because they had some kind of inherent power.

Rather than approaching this book as authorities or experts, we reread all of the interviews we had conducted over the years, and came to the same conclusion all fans do: the best thing to do would be to shut up and listen. We did add other information to broaden the sense of context, but mainly we wanted to sit back and enjoy the diversity and breadth of what we'd been told, face to face, by so many different rappers. We've tried to select and frame the quotes without skewing or dominating the conversation.

Like rap music itself, this book is meant to be enjoyed with the volume cranked up. Like a head-bobbing beat, it's something to drench yourself in, something that has its own unique logic, rhythm, and science. To borrow a phrase from KRS-One, it's a little unrational, and needn't be read in any particular order. It was assembled not in the hope that readers would walk away with a single, rational definition of what hip-hop means, but that through these words and pictures they would immerse themselves in what rap feels like, be inspired to return to their stereos and enjoy it directly, deep down in their bones.

—Gregor and Dimitri Ehrlich

17

DROPPING
SCIENCE

"Throughout history technology has destroyed civilization. And it's time for civilization to take back civilization. When technology rules civilization, you have false politics and false school systems and atomic weapons and all kinds of things that destroy civilization. When civilization is in control of technology, you have medicine, you have philosophy, art, music, things that help humanity along. But we don't realize this and as a result we're becoming more of a technological society and not a civilization."

—KRS-One

"I feel that once the black man gets himself better situated, the pyramids will be nothing compared to what this generation is gonna do."

—Lord Jamar, Brand Nubian

"It's really easy to say something in a song, and it's another thing to be responsible and put into action what you say. That's where I feel that WE GAIN STRENGTH, through constantly conquering our own shortcomings and questioning our own beliefs."

—Michael Franti, Disposable Heroes of Hiphoprisy

"The way we came up with the name Main Source is that we feel that the **PEOPLE ARE THE MAIN SOURCE OF THIS PLANET,** right? And we're just a representation of the people."

—The Large Professor, Main Source

"Capitalism might be the wicked game, but we're caught up in the middle of it. So **WE BETTER MAKE UP OUR OWN RULES,** with some capitalism in it, some Marxism, some Afrocentrism. The only way to change problems isn't necessarily a violent revolution, but a revolution in education at least."

—Chuck D, Public Enemy

21

"**A LOT OF PEOPLE ARE AFRAID.** They have stars and icons because they're afraid to tell themselves that they're worth a lot fucking more than they think they are. As much as people respect other artists, they should feel that respect within themselves. I don't really separate myself or put myself on another level from the people that surround me. And it should be that way with everybody."

—Prince Be, PM Dawn

"I felt that I needed something in my life that was spiritually grounding, that I could lean on. I didn't have anything so I chose Islam."

—Q-Tip, A Tribe Called Quest

A TRIBE CALLED QUEST ▶

"There are about 1.4 million (527,000 adults) Muslims in the United States, 40% of whom are African-Americans. Only a fraction are believed to identify with the Five Percent sect."

— Barry A. Kosmin, City University of New York

"**FIVE PERCENT** don't deal with hatred, Five Percent deals with the truth. **THE NATURE OF WHITE MAN IS DEVIL-ISHNESS. THE NATURE OF BLACK PEOPLE IS ORIGINAL, GOD-LIKE.** The first life-form found in existence on the planet was a black man, the first destructive element that was created was by a white man. Society as we know it, history as it has been recorded, the information that has been channeled out to condition the minds of the masses, has been designed by the agendas of white men."

—Busta Rhymes

"When we speak of the devil we're not just trying to attack white people, we're talking about the devilish mentality. The devil is within the black man. The black man was first and the white man was second. That means he came from us, we created that devilish mentality."

—Lord Jamar, Brand Nubian

The radical Five Percent Nation of Islam is a small North American Muslim sect that takes its name from the belief that only 5% of the black population has a true awareness of the role of blacks in history and the oppression facing blacks today. Its doctrine includes the belief that whites are "devils."

— Los Angeles Times, 1991

"When you're in this line of duty—which is teaching the science of a civilized person to uncivilized people, in the wilderness of North America—you're subject to these temporary injustices. In a land I consider based on lies, **THE WORST ENEMY TO WHITE PEOPLE WOULD BE WHAT? THE TRUTH.** Ain't nobody tellin' the truth. Everybody is based on a lie. That the black man ain't nothin' but a slave. And before he has a slave he was runnin' wild in Swahili somewhere, jumpin' around out of trees, doin' flips on **rhinoceros' backs** with bones in his noses. That is totally ill. Black man is the father of the oldest civilization ever to exist on planet Earth."

—Wise Intelligent, Poor Righteous Teachers

"**ISLAM** means **I** **S**elf **L**ord **A**nd **M**aster. If I live according to that, I can't be wrong. Long as I stay peaceful. **How could you be God with hatred?** Just 'cause I don't point the finger at people and put the sword over their head, doesn't mean I'm not a 5 percenter."

—Rakim

"**Ignorance**
is an enemy
that is created
by the enemy."

—Busta Rhymes

"If Nelson Mandela can survive what he went
through, and if Winnie Mandela can survive what
they both went through, that proves that BLACK
PEOPLE CAN SURVIVE ANYTHING because of
our strength and our power. And what we all
need to do is take our love and our power and
share it amongst everybody. And this whole world
will unite together and build a force so strong
nobody can tear it down."

—Flavor Flav

"I tell every interviewer who asks me why
I'm not Afrocentric that I'm from New York,
for God's sake! I wasn't born in Africa!
**I DON'T KNOW ANYTHING ABOUT AFRICA,
EXCEPT WHAT I SEE ON PBS!"**

—Shazzy

"School is not structured for the multicultural
experience. It's only structured for Europeans.
That structure doesn't work for the millions
of other cultures that exist. The **so-called
minorities** in America can't identify with
the Eurocentric ideal."

—MC Dinko D, Leaders of the New School

"I once read a book that said a lotus could
grow and bloom in the midst of a swamp. Can't
nobody stop me. If I'm in the midst of darkness,
I'm still gonna bloom, because **I am the lotus
in the swamp of New York."**

—Smooth B, Nice and Smooth

CRIMINAL
MINDED

SIMI VALLEY, Calif., April 29—Four Los Angeles police officers were acquitted of assault today in the videotaped beating of a black motorist that stunned the nation. The verdicts immediately touched off a storm of anger and scattered violence in the city.

As residents set scores of fires, looted stores, and beat passing motorists in the downtown area and pockets of predominantly black south-central Los Angeles, Mayor Tom Bradley declared a state of emergency, and Gov. Pete Wilson said he would send in the National Guard.

After hearing seven weeks of detailed testimony and studying the 81-second amateur videotape of the beating, the jury concluded that the policemen, all of whom are white, had not broken any laws when they clubbed and kicked the mostly prone motorist, Rodney G. King.

—*The New York Times*, April 30, 1992

"GENERATIONS OF NOT GIVING A FUCK IS WHAT LED UP TO ALL OF THIS.

There were two platforms during the L.A. riots—one repre sented by Rodney King, the other by George Bush. Bush came out to all the masses, all the scared white people, and said, "We will restore order, I guarantee that. I got 2,000 Marines, 1,000 state troopers," all that. What he's really saying is, "I got $20 billion here, $45 million here, and $3 billion there." That's what he's saying to the corporations. And to the black people he's saying, **"We're gonna kill you nigger!** Nigger! Listen! You burned down all this shit; we're coming for your ass right now. Here's the Marines on your ass right now." And then comes Rodney King with, **'We can get along, we can live together.'** I was in L.A. the next day; you wouldn't believe the unity, the love, the respect. We're battling with how we feel, versus how it is. How it is, is that we've got to pick up knives and just start killing. How we feel is that someday, one day, we'll get along with each other in some sort of harmony and equilibrium. That's how black people feel."

—KRS-One

"One thing that got ignored about the L.A. riots is the Bloods and Crips. **THE BIGGEST THING EVERY BLACK PERSON WANTS TO SEE IS AN END TO FEAR IN OUR OWN LIVES.** If the Bloods and Crips stop killing each other, but when you saw the news, gangs coming together was seen as some kind of side issue, when for us it was the biggest issue in the world. . . Before the L.A. riots, Hollywood would slide that shit out: *Juice*, *Boyz N the Hood*. It shows the difference between the two worlds, and how far that other world is from our world. Before, it was just a money maker, and it was all just a joke. Now they see that what we are saying on these tapes is becoming a reality. Everybody is steppin' back."

—Parrish Smith, EpMd

"We all die from something anyway, and I'd rather go out like a hero than a sucker. I'd rather go out like Malcolm X than go out like Jesse Jackson."

—KRS-One

"Malcolm's agenda was human rights and self-determination. Free people have a right to self-determination, self-defense. Now, a lot of people say, 'Self-defense? Oh, my God, that's violence.' If people think 'by any means necessary' means violence, what that says is that that individual is violent and hostile. But not my husband."

—Dr. Betty Shabazz

"Peace is a means and violence is a means. Self-defense is part of survival. If violence is needed in order to survive then that's what needs to be done. If things can be settled in a peaceful way then that's the way it should be done, but Malcolm X said, 'By any means necessary.'"

—Lord Jamar

"To pit Dr. King's philosophy of nonviolence against Malcolm's purported creed of violence is a distortion of Malcolm's position. Malcolm consistently talked self-defense. The media distorted the argument."

—A. Peter Bailey,
former member of Malcolm X's
Organization of Afro-American Unity

"I think in self-defense, **violence** is called intelligence. If something seeks to **hurt you** and you **protect yourself,** that's being intelligent. If you turn the other cheek, that's ignorance, because that's not a natural act. **If one animal bites another animal, they're gonna fight."**

—Ice Cube ▸

"There might be a time when there will be a **call to arms.** I'm not preaching that everybody should get a gun and go wild, but there's gonna be a time when the black man is gonna need a force also."

—Sadat X, Brand Nubian

"**'HOW I COULD JUST KILL A MAN'** was written for people who don't understand, and that ain't the kids in the ghetto. That's for the people who sit back and read the newspapers, and watch the news on TV about domestic violence in the ghettos and ask, 'Why are these kids killing each other?' You don't know unless you live it. If somebody wants to take my life, I ain't gonna let 'em."

—DJ Muggs, Cypress Hill

"I'm not all about violence, I'm about being myself. **I just write about what I've been through on the streets** because it's really the only thing I've ever known."

—G Lock

"Black America is tired of having their brothers and sisters murdered by the police for no reason other than being black. I'm not advocating violence. I'm saying I can understand it. If the people are frustrated and feel oppressed and feel this is the only way they can act, I understand."

—Spike Lee

"We deal with the gang problems day-to-day. We drive down the street and get sweated every day. So many gangs around there. When you see it every day, it's normal."

37

—DJ Muggs, Cypress Hill

"I find when you're truthful with the people, and you're not just writin' it for the hardcore image or for the money, they respect it. Because when we do shows, although our songs are hardcore, we talk to the people. It's like, "O.K., we're hearing some violent type shit, but it ain't just about violence. It's about you learning about situations that you can avoid."

—B. Real, Cypress Hill

"RAPPERS ARE TALKING ABOUT CRIME BECAUSE THEY SEE IT EVERY DAY or they hear about it. We're all involved, and it's good to have a couple songs about what you see, but not the whole album. If every time you come out you're rapping about literally ducking bullets when you go to the store to get a carton of milk—it's not like that."

—Rakim

"We used to break up the monotony of all the tension building up in the neighborhood. 'Cause there was a lot of times where the only event that everyone had was gangs. Before we were on radio, we would go around to each town, and we would hold parties in the park, and hold 'em hostage, and make 'em have a good time."

—Flavor Flav

"When I have on my rapping face, I portray a hardcore image. YOU CAN'T BE ALL SOFT AND RAP HARD, you just can't do it. It's like that with Cube. When he has on his rapping face, it's hard and he never goes out of character. Some people judge a book by its cover."

—Yo-Yo

◀ FLAVOR FLAV

39

"Nobody would go to see
ARNOLD SCHWARZENEGGER'S
movie if it was a lollipop
movie. People want to
see action, so we give
'em action."

—B. Real, Cypress Hill

"As far as kids buying my record goes, their parents can
look at me and say, HERE'S A WHITE KID, and they automatically think I'm a clean-cut guy. But I'm not clean-cut.
I've been through all kinds of shit on the streets, I got
stabbed, I've stolen cars—stuff I'm not proud of. People
can't accept that a white kid did grow up in the streets.
I'm expressing myself through rap music no
matter what color I am."

—Vanilla Ice

"When I used to come downtown on the weekend with my mother and father, it used to be so hot that you took out the mattress on the fire escape and just lounged. Sleep out there and nobody would bother you, leave your door open. The regular local store was open 24-7, and you could just walk in, not just up to a window. This was on 111th Street between 7th and 8th Avenue in Harlem. You could be out all day all night playing ball, enjoying yourself. **TODAY, YOU GOT TO WATCH YOUR BACK,** you can't open to everybody, you got to keep everything locked. You can't be free to everybody. Everybody tend to take from you. Everybody envy you."

—**Kool DJ Red Alert**

41

"We did a commercial for St. Ide's Malt Liquor, because we write about what's goin' down with the type of crowd we hang with. We do what we need to do, to keep us happy. But by the same token, when we do our tours we say, "Just Say No" to try to inspire kids."

—**Erick Sermon, EpMd**

"I didn't come out against people doing beer ads. I came out against the companies for promoting those ads in black neighborhoods, trying to say that they are not targeting blacks. There's a two-mile strip in Louisville—I think it's called Muhammad Ali Boulevard—and every other block has a billboard: Newport, Old English, PowerMaster, St. Ide's, and they still say they don't target black audiences. Try finding that in a white area. Companies that don't stand a chance to do well all over concentrate on the black community, because the black community doesn't have the power to say, "Get that shit the fuck outta here!" But when shit starts burnin' down, they start listenin'. They start cancelin' movies. I read in the paper that Hollywood is thinking about censoring some movies because they start other riots. All because of the L.A. riots."

—Chuck D, Public Enemy

43

"We all know
the war on drugs
is a joke."
—KRS-One

"As soon as they see you wearing GOLD CHAINS and JEWELRY, and driving a fancy car, they automatically think you're a DRUG DEALER."

—Howie Tee, producer

◀ B. REAL, CYPRESS HILL

"Being in prison was the same thing as being at home, as far as writing goes. I have ideas in my mind and I just match the lyrics to the music, the same as I used to when I was at home."

—Slick Rick

"We wore Adidas sneakers with no shoelaces, we got that idea from prison. We always got our ideas from the outside world and incorporated them in what we were doing."

—Run, RUN-DMC ▶

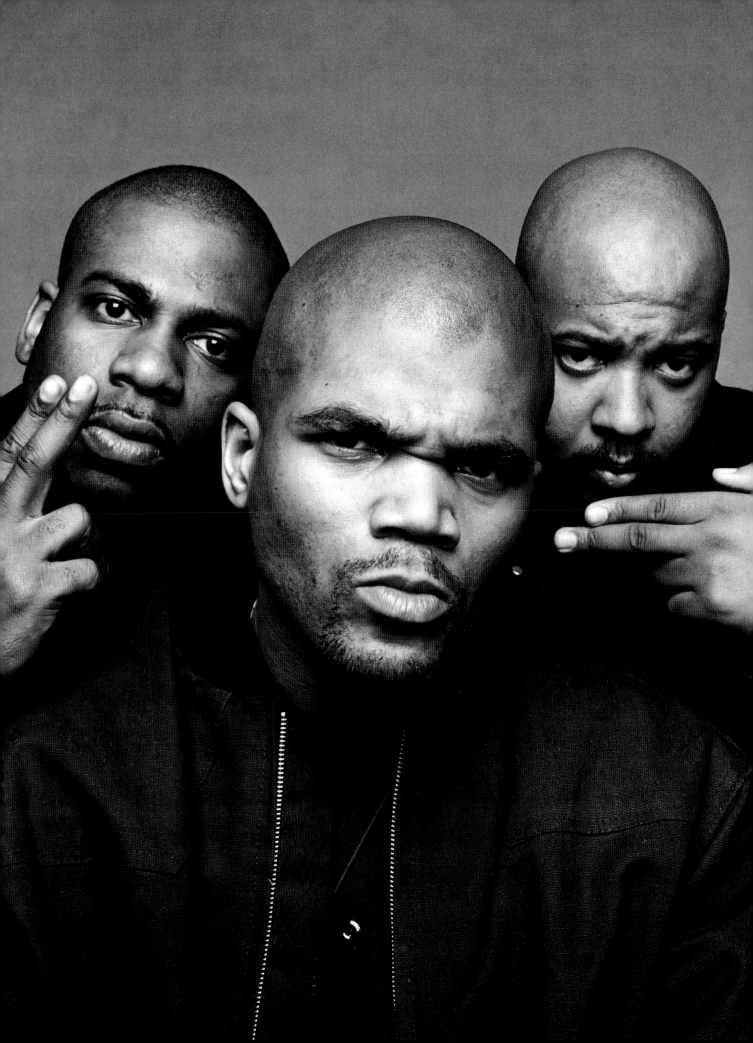

Since 1990 alone, the number of prison and jail guards nation-wide has increased by about 30 percent, to more than 600,000. . . . California, with the largest number of prisoners, is facing the biggest challenge. In the last 20 years, California has built 21 new prisons but added only one university to what was once hailed as the world's best public university system. And while the share of the state budget going to the university system has fallen to 8 per-cent from 12.5 percent in 1990, the proportion for corrections has risen to 9.4 percent, up 4.5 percent, an amount that educators point out is identical to the loss in their funds. In the meantime, California's universities have had to lay off 10,000 employees, many of them professors, while in the same period the number of state prison guards has increased by 10,000.

—*The New York Times*, September 28, 1997

"YOU PUT A GUY IN JAIL WHEN HE THIRTEEN, YOU LET HIM OUT WHEN HE TWENTY-TWO YEARS OLD, WHAT YOU EXPECT FOR HIM TO BE? You can't expect for him to come out smart, and expect him to adapt to the Earth, the way things is. By being incarcerated you lose so much knowledge of the world, man, your social knowledge, you lose that, that's gone, all you have is the incarcerated mentality, and that's all we grew up around: brothers who just came out. It's weird because the generations carry on. There's guys fifty-five years old, still campaignin', running around these streets and gang-banging with guys fifteen years old. That's all they know. If you been to jail for twenty-two years and they just let you out today, you ain't got nowhere to live, half your family died, you ain't knowin' nothin'. Your knowledge could be snatched from you so fast, man, that's what everybody fights for now: they spirit and they mind. And if they don't find it, boy, they gonna be in a lot of trouble. **BECAUSE IT'S CRUCIAL OUT HERE, AND IT'S A CONFLICT WITH THE WHOLE PLANET."**

—**Cold Hard, Crucial Conflict**

47

"Unless America awakens to the fact that she must contend with us as an enemy or bargain with us as citizens, it will be to her serious disadvantage."

—Maulana Karenga

MAKE WAY FOR THE MOTHERLODE

"Guys come up all the time and say, 'Hey baby, I could take you in my house and feed you and clothe you.' Well, I can do that for myself. What else can you do for me? Benefit my emotional and mental health. That might be upping the ante. But they better watch out because bitches, ho's—whatever you want to call us— we're not having it. We're on the uprise."

—Nikki D

"We felt that it would be better for our safety not to be walking around looking like bitches. So we wouldn't put on any makeup, just throw on some baggy clothes, 'cause if were dressed like bitches, they'd be talking about raping us. When we first got out to L.A., we had no idea it was gonna be that way. PEOPLE KILL ME WHEN THEY COME UP AND SAY, 'YOU LOOK LIKE A DYKE ON YOUR ALBUM COVER.' Well, I don't give a fuck what you think I look like. If she had been in my situation, she probably wouldn't have had enough common sense to dress down. She would have just gone back home and quit."

—The Boss

THE BOSS, AND HER PARTNER, DEE ▶

"I see little girls saying, 'You ain't fucking with this bitch.' **Now they calling *theyself* bitch!** It's becoming cool to do that. That's not right."

—Rakim

"We're not putting down women, It's just street talk. Women understand that. They like us. They buy our records. They don't think of us as bad guys. That's just how you talk about women."

—M.C. Ren

"Especially after my album hit, it got so easy, with all these bitches who want to throw themselves at me. It's like they have a lack of respect for themselves. So that's why I use word 'bitch' and 'ho' so fluidly."

—DJ Quik

"I'm fed up with women, to tell you the honest truth. They're so materialistic, I just want to say to them, Can't you go out and make your own money, instead of trying to juice me for mine when I'm asleep? I've been with women who take my clothing while I sleep! I caught up to this one girl, and she stole my hat and my pager! Just so that she could see me again."

—Mellow Man Ace

53

"Somebody has to take a stand, because nobody is being a leader. Everybody's on this bandwagon mentality, now everybody wants to beat up a girl— everybody thinks a girl is a bitch. It's like, don't you have sisters? Don't you have mothers? And is 'bitch' what you call them? In my opinion, if you want to consider yourself a motherfucker or a nigger, keep it to yourself. Don't teach girls they should be bitches, and don't teach guys they should be niggers. I never noticed it before, but now I'm really starting to see how easily led they are. All this war between the sexes stuff is played out, but the media tends to glamorize, glorify and blow up situations, in order to make it more appealing."

—Queen Latifah

"I think women in hip-hop have stood back long enough. Foxy Brown, Lil' Kim and Da Brat are proving that women can sell a million albums, so now everyone wants a woman in their camp. I'm just trying to make a record that's global."

—Charli Baltimore

"I've been on tour with Big Daddy Kane, right? When I come back to the hotel at the end of the show I see 50 million girls campin' out in the hallways, waitin' to get into Kane's room."

—Monie Love

BIG DADDY KANE ▶

"Our shit is sexual I think, but it's just more classy. Like an old 1940s movie rather than a 1990s movie."

—Q-Tip, A Tribe Called Quest

"That **sex symbol** thing ain't real. I could go through a windshield and that shit would be **over**. My music has to stand up on the radio. A cute guy comes out every five minutes."

—L.L. Cool J

"Everyone asked me if I argue with Cube about sexism. And I say, I don't believe in fighting fire with fire, because it just gets hotter. I believe in being classy but sassy."

—Yo-Yo

MC LYTE ▶

"Ice Cube is the coolest person on earth to me. The very same one talkin' about bitches. I knew him before he did the album, and then when I got the album I was like, 'Whoa.' Yet he still treats me with the same respect that he always did."

—Monie Love

"At first, of course I was offended by the five-letter word [bitch]. As I got more involved with rap and met a lot of rappers, I realized that they respected me, and that they weren't talking about me. And there are women out there who can be bitchy, I'm not denying that. There are girls out there who are gold-diggers and it's natural that rappers are gonna talk about that."

—Yo-Yo

"A lot of the things that feminists have done are very important, but my point is that the media always wants to categorize people. I'm black, you know? I don't need to be called a 'black feminist.'"

—Queen Latifah

IT'S NOT ABOUT A SALARY, IT'S ALL ABOUT REALITY

"Oral expressive culture—rap poetry, for example, and the customs of 'signifying' and playing the 'dozens'—still surrounds the written tradition almost like a Mobius strip, in a way reminiscent of the traditional antiphonal 'call-and-response' structures peculiar to African and African-American culture. A visit today to a beauty parlor or barbershop in a black neighborhood easily verifies that this oral, dialectical tradition is alive and well."

—Henry Louis Gates Jr.

"You have to be one with your audience. That's technique 'A.' 'A' is not to do hip-hop but to be hip-hop. When you're one with the art form that you represent, then you're one with the people that are a part of that art form."

—KRS-One

"Rapping comes from the street, doo-wop comes from the street. We bring these together to show that to young people. Our goal is to show that rapping is the basics."

—Easy Moe Bee

"A lot of people think that when you do rock and rap you are more into the pop side of things. They don't realize that black artists were the architects of rock 'n' roll."

—Chubb Rock

63

"The golden age of hip-hop to me is when Eric B. and Rakim had "Check Out My Melody," when KRS had "Criminal Minded," just before L.L. had "Mama Said Knock You Out." Real hip-hop shit. To me, hip-hop artists then were superstars. To me that was when hip-hop was just bigger than life. Today, you seen one rapper, you seen 'em all. Back then, they came with a complete show, the whole art form of hip-hop was serious."

—Fat Joe the Gangsta

"Hip-hop was something that sprouted out from nothing. It was like God must have said, here's something for y'all to make some money. As long as you do good with it, you'll be alright."

—Slick Rick

"**THE '88 ERA,** with Rakim and Kane was one of the most inspiring eras of my life. It was just incredible because it was clean and **it was all about hip-hop.** Nowadays the politics overweigh the music. Back then, **it was about your skills and your beats.**"

—Peter Gunz

"People want **variety** in rap. A lot of new artists won't be around long if they don't start to talk about **other things** besides, 'I'm-a shoot you, I'm-a kill your mother and stab your family.' **Nobody can be angry all the time.** Audiences wanna go back to things that made them **laugh and feel good.** A lot of older artists' stuff is still in style."

—Doug E. Fresh

"In the early days, rap wasn't as popular as it is now, but the message was the same. **ALL RAP IS SAYING ONE THING: 'I AM SOMEBODY.'** That hasn't changed."

—Larry Smith, producer of RUN-DMC

What began in the grim housing projects of New York over a decade ago has affected the style, fashion and slang of a much wider society. Rap jingles sell goods, rap videos sell television shows, a rap album sold 7 million copies this year (more than any of the big-name stars). Commercial rap cuts across race and class as the music—and culture—of young America. It can be heard in shopping malls and on street corners. At one end of the spectrum are the hardcore 'gangster rappers,' . . . particularly a west coast phenomenon. There, rap started late, and the gang culture remains strong. These lyrics depict ice-cold killers with gold chains swaggering in a desolate wasteland. This, they argue, is the reality of their ghetto existence. But their love affair with weapons, and the middle-class rappers who pretend to be gangsters, suggest that they are depicting violence for the sake of it. Their message goes down as well in white suburbs as in the inner cities.

The Economist, December 8, 1990

"It's good that we're getting a lot more exposure now. It's like you see ice cream men on cereal boxes rapping. So it's good that it's universal now. It's major. We have to be in the public's eyes."

—Rakim

"You see these **dime a dozen** rappers and this is what they look like: jeans, sweatshirt, and a gold chain. Pick up 50 million record covers and you'll see that. **But that's what sells records.**"

—Monie Love ▸

"Instead of being trifling to your people, you can do right by your people. But the only way to deal with the motherfuckers is to **capture their ass and recondition their mindstates.** As far as commercialization, I don't give a fuck about that, I'm real cool if I get it, but my agenda is to make sure that people feel my music like at the end of the day. Commercialization is cool but **I'M NOT TRYING TO ADJUST MY SHIT TO BE COMMERCIAL.** Like, I can't go to that 'cause that's not what my initial agenda is, you know what I'm saying? My initial agenda is to be honored as one of the most contributive in this art. Credibly."

—Busta Rhymes

"It doesn't even **faze me** that they have rap in **Pepsi** commercials."

—Ice Cube

"Some people were **offended** by **Ice Cube's** lyrics, but I was offended by the music. About 60% of all rap records that come out offend me, because they're so **musically sleepin'**. That bothers me much more than the commercialization of rap. **What it comes down to is, who's making creative music?**"

—Mike D., the Beastie Boys

"There are many writers out there who are not really that familiar with hip-hop who can come up with a fly chorus, can come up with lyrics that can pass, and they can even sell a million records. But I'm thinking that, in music, you wanna be like Paul McCartney."

—Chubb Rock

"I have little bass lines in my head, pretty much at all times."

—Ant Banks

"Most of my stuff is sampled. I really don't play nothin'. I don't just loop things, I chop a lot sounds up. I think all of rap is getting more musical now. Not so much more live playing, but more musical loops. It ain't all about big kick drums and eerie sounds and shit like that. It's more melodic. Personally, I listen to a lot of jazz, like Miles Davis, Donald Levy, that kind of stuff. SOMETHING FUNKY COULD COME FROM ANYWHERE, MAN. You'd be surprised where we find the funkiest shit: movie soundtracks . . . I found some Hungarian music that's mad funky!"

—JuJu, the Beatnuts

"I was like, yo! I have a concept. We all love R&B but we all listen to hip-hop. Imagine someone just singing on top of those beats we love. But I never imagined it would take off so big."

—Puff Daddy

"Now that every sample has to be cleared, it's gonna be something only really rich bands can do. Whereas the whole thing that originally appealed to us about rap was the same thing that appealed to us about punk, which is part of the aesthetic of the music: that anyone can do it. For me, sampling was a great extension of that."

—Mike D., the Beastie Boys

"I told all of the producers that I didn't want samples because I felt that the producers tended to depend too much on samples. We need to be more creative, as opposed to sitting there and taking everybody else's stuff; we need to make the things that will become samples in the future."

—Queen Latifah

"The first think I look for in an artist is personality. We're very much into a rock 'n' roll attitude. I like things that are hectic."

—Hank Shocklee, producer, Public Enemy

"With rap they try to pigeonhole you but everyone has a split personality. People try to make you one thing or another: hardcore or pop—but it's not like that. I'm a diverse person and I've always been that way. It's the sights and sounds and smells of it that you have to capture to be a great rapper and bring listeners into the story. So they can close their eyes and it's almost like they're there."

—Jay-Z

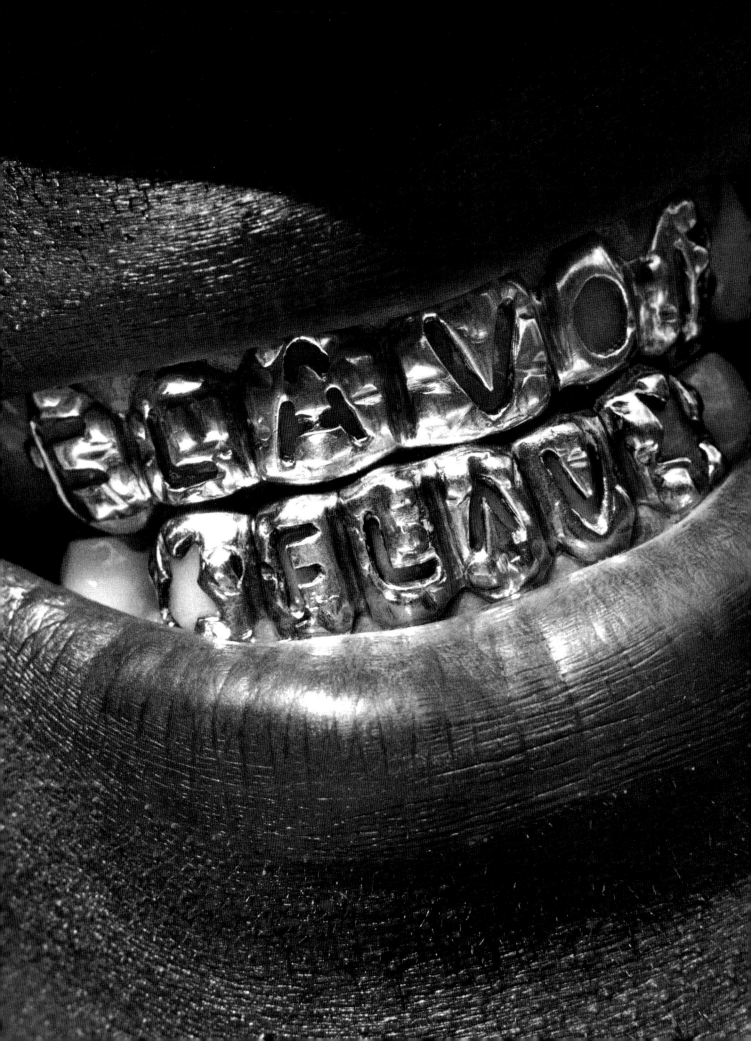

"My definition of **conscious rap** is lyrics that make somebody aware of something we do everyday that might not be 100% right."

—Rakim

"Conscious rap got diluted because people were doing it so much that listeners were getting bored and wanted to hear something different. KRS-One knew how to do it in a way where he also entertained you. Just like Public Enemy. You would have Chuck D. giving you information but it didn't bore you because you had Flavor Flav on the side being humorous and comical. So you have to learn how to balance that. When conscious rap came out, everybody jumped on the bandwagon, but then when L.L. Cool J came out with 'Jinglin' Baby' people said **'I'm tired of hearing that conscious stuff. Let's party now.'**"

—Kool DJ Red Alert

◀ FLAVOR FLAV

"It's stupid for somebody to say rap is dead, because it teaches you something now. . . But message rap has been around for a long time, too, like [Grandmaster Flash's 1984 recording] **"The Message,"** for example—and that's still getting played. See, but I can't sit there and make a whole album full of messages, because then I don't have any fun. **I'm not a scholar or professor, so I can't make a whole album full of teaching, 'cause I'm still learning."**

—Queen Latifah ›

"We write about people who grow up in the ghettos and the stereotype that to have success you have to be a musician, athlete, or a drug dealer. **We want to show that a person coming out of the ghetto has the same potential as someone coming out of Beverly Hills, if you put your mind to it."**

—Large Professor, Main Source

"One thing rap music has done is make people look at words differently than 20 years ago. Take rap language—like the other day some white kid called into this cable math show like, "Yo, yo, yo, run that back." And the teacher didn't know which way to turn."

—Chuck D

"There's no way a word can change the way a person behaves. It's each person's responsibility not to let negative words like "bitch" change your whole attitude. It's up to you. You gotta fight it."

—Hurricane, The Afros

"A lot of kids talk about, 'Oh, I want to be a rap singer,' and they cut school to go to the nearest park and sit down and start rappin' with their friends. But they don't realize that—I mean, **no matter what you want to do, school is crazy important.** If there was one thing I ever paid attention to in school it was English! That was my favorite subject. Your lyrical content, your knowledge of words—different words and different meanings, and stuff like that—it's real intricate!"

—Monie Love

"We always sit down and try to make up some **new words.** It just proves that **people are tired of using the same old words,** so we come up with new words. That's just the **street.**"

—Hurricane, the Afros

"We just write rhymes and if people listen they can learn. **People shouldn't look to rap as a replacement for books.** Literacy is unbelievably low. Sit down and pick up a book. A book is going to touch your life more than any song. I give people enough credit that they can think and learn for themselves."

—Pete Nice, 3rd Bass

"Rap is just a way for us youngsters to tell a story, the same way the elders of the tribe used to tell stories from generation to generation. Rap is just a language for expression of what has happened from generation to generation. But you know that you can relate to a wider crowd if you just add some **dope beats** when you tell your story."

—Chip-Fu, the Fu-Schnickens

"I'm not a role model, because I'm still in here building, I'm still young. But a lot of people I encounter need direction, and I want to tell them that **success isn't what it was painted to be.** Very few get to come back and talk about it. There's a heavy price to pay, and I think that's what needs to be emphasized. As far as the music goes, I think that speaks for itself."

—Parrish Smith, EpMd

"Hopefully we can spread the message and bring back the 'fro. Back in the '60s, everybody had an afro, from the coolest guy on the corner to the powerful political leaders. So we're trying to get back with that vibe."

—Hurricane, the Afros

"When I was in school I was a 'Z' student. **I learned the most when I left school.** At that time I was thirteen, and I was homeless, so I would use the library as a shelter. I would just sit there and read. I believe kids should learn what they want to learn, what's relevant to them in today's society."

—KRS-One

"During the 1960s when you had the Motown sound they were just giving you details of what life was revolving around during the years of the Vietnam War. Also there were riots going on in various cities. But I was not really into it until later on when I started learning about what was going on musically at that time. I was listening to people like Sly and the Family Stone, Curtis Mayfield, Marvin Gaye. I hate to say it but a lot of people do not do their homework. I think those records made back in the '60s were giving us the news: that was our newspaper. It was teaching us what to stay away from and what to do to make things better for ourselves. But the people of today, they've taken it a different route.

—Kool DJ Red Alert

"I don't put myself on any higher plane just because a lot of people listen to my music. It's just a job, like a mailman. I don't think people should put on me the pressure of raising kids all over the country. I don't think I should be the mother and father. I think the mother and father should be the mother and father."

—Ice Cube

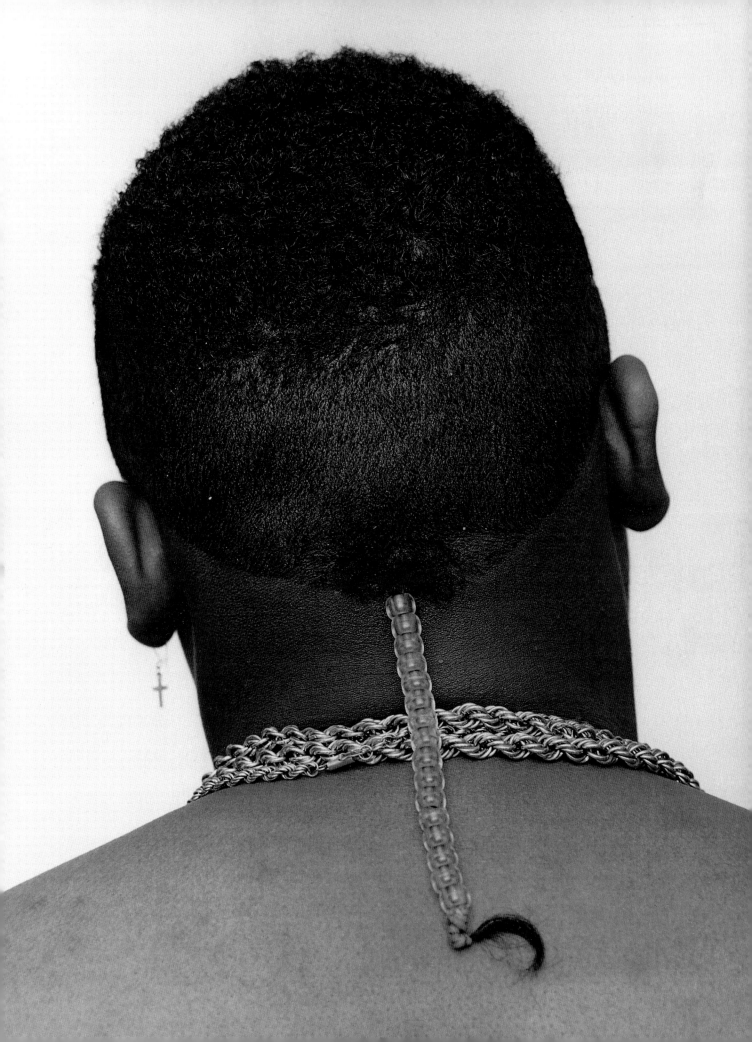

WHAT'S the 4-1-1? Or, for the culturally deprived, what's happening? Glocks (semi-automatic weapons) and gangbangin'—that's what's happening, and slangin' and early death. Hip-hop's recent adventures have been so chilling that even its founders are concerned about its future. The music is still young—so young most of its veterans haven't yet hit 40. And some of its stars never will. The recent violent deaths of rappers Tupac Shakur and the Notorious B.I.G., a.k.a. Biggie Smalls, a.k.a, Christopher Wallace, and thousands of other children without big names or lucrative record contracts have led analysts, industry officials and rappers to step back and, as they say, recognize.

—*Ebony*, June 1997

"As a true artist, you should never edit your creativity. If you feel something, you should right it. Put it out. Practice it. Know it. It's a part of you. It's your art. Being a true artist also means just representing yourself. But when you want that art to sell, you enter a realm called strategy, in which you will edit yourself. So in one area I would say, 'Yes, you have to censor yourself as an artist.' But on the other hand, to be a true artist, you should never censor yourself. It's really the distance you've got to take your art."

—KRS-One ▸

"My record company is scared of MTV or something. They call MTV and tell them every video I'm about to do. I wanted to do a video for 'The Product' and 'Endangered Species.' My record company sent them the lyrics and they almost went through the roof. That ain't justifying rap music and it ain't getting the music out there. MTV is just like all the others: they on the bandwagon. MTV is not needed, for one thing, for us to get our message across, and I'm never gonna do another video for MTV ever. Never."

—Ice Cube

"Censorship almost provokes you to listen to that shit. You want to see what's in the album because parents say you shouldn't."

—Shazzy

"When I saw the big CENSORSHIP stickers on 2 Live Crew's album it drove me from not carin' about the music to trying desperately to find out exactly what was being said."

—Monie Love

"We shouldn't outlaw the records they make. We should outlaw the conditions to which they point. The Rodney King riots show us we are always just one step from Armageddon in the ghetto. The attempt by American culture to sweep so many of the problems of the inner city under the rug, out of sight, has come back with a vengeance through the voice of rap musicians, especially the more politically conscious."

—Michael Dyson, African-American
Professor of Ethics and Cultural Criticism
at Chicago Theological Seminary.
Seattle Times, May 12, 1992

"There isn't a doubt in my mind that my husband would still be alive if Tupac hadn't written these violent, anti-police songs and the companies involved hadn't published and put them out on the street," said Davidson, tugging at her husband's wedding band, which dangled from a gold chain around her neck. "I'm sure Tupac has no feeling for me or what happened to my husband. He obviously has a great anger toward law enforcement. All he cares about is singing his songs and making his money, no matter who he hurts." — Linda Sue Davidson, wife of slain California State Trooper Bill Davidson, killed by Ronald Ray Howard, who was reportedly listening to *2PACALYPSE NOW* at the time of the incident.

—October 13, 1992, *Los Angeles Times*

"I don't think it's a matter of censorship. Gosh, it's a public collection, us taxpayers own the cassettes and books that are in that collection. We should have a say about what's in the collection. Does that mean I'm censoring this group? I don't think so. You can't blame (N. W. A's music) on the central L.A. core or downtown Seattle or whatever central district you want to talk about. One of the librarians said, 'Well, this is black America, this is black culture.' I said, 'Whoa, wait a minute, that has nothing to do with black culture, it has nothing to do with hard life on the streets.' This is obscenity to me."

—Michael Caldwell, Executive Administrative Assistant
for the city of Lynwood, Oregon, whose library voted to ban an
N.W.A album from its collection, *Seattle Times*, May 12, 1992

"Motherfucking underground music is the core of the hip-hop fabric. At the end of the day if your shit flops on a commercial level, you still have your credibility in the street."

—Busta Rhymes

Time Warner Inc. is reviewing its investment in Interscope Records as controversy continues over Warner Music's involvement in distributing rap music with violent lyrics. Time Warner owns 50 percent of Interscope, which has distributed gangster rap artists such as Tupac Shakur, Dr. Dre and Snoop Doggy Dog. Gangster rap is considered among the most offensive rap music by its critics. Time Warner has been singled out by Sen. Robert Dole, who is seeking the Republican nomination for president, for distributing rap music with violent lyrics.

—Associated Press, June 6, 1995

"The first time it's just so exciting to be involved with making a record, it's almost like a dream. **One day I was a messenger, the next day I was touring with Bobby Brown,** meeting the Jacksons, and working with Larry Blackmon from Cameo."

—Smooth B, Nice and Smooth

"I'm a person about **change.** There's so much money in the hip-hop industry right now that **people shouldn't be struggling.** There should be seesaws in the parks and books in the schools. **We have the tools to make a change. We make records, but we don't make changes.**"

—Queen Pen

"I still live in the same neighborhood, still tend to people the same way. I feel better that way because I feel you'll be more respected when people see you don't change. A lot of people expect you to be fancy, riding big cars, living in a big house. I don't that think really gives you respect. Just remain as you are."

—Kool DJ Red Alert ▶

"I never had any problems in my neighborhood. I've been around when there are shootings going on, and whatever. **But I never got caught in a crossfire.** There's no reason for me to leave. If it's supposed to take me five minutes to get from here to there and it takes me half an hour because I got to go around the violence, that's when I'll leave."

—Howie Tee, producer for UTFO, Full Force, Chubb Rock

"We **enjoying ourselves.** Whether if somebody dead, or not. We got to **celebrate,** man, because times is shorter than anybody ever could think. **Death is the only thing guaranteed.** We gonna keep trying to make it, no matter how much people try to take us down. We not gonna act like we all special. We gonna be the same people all our lives. I could be famous, our name could ring a bell for life! But when I walk down the street people gonna see me and say, hey there. Because they gonna say man, **he stayed in the 'hood.**"

—Cold Hard, Crucial Conflict

"I go off on my little thing and do what I wanna do, but **I never forget where I came from.**"

—Queen Latifah

The most dangerous myth facing African-Americans today is that middle-class life is counterfeit and that only poverty and suffering, and the rage that attends them, are real. When middle-class blacks fabricate violent urban pasts, they pay homage to murder. When record company executives pose for pictures with gun-toting rappers, and when they push that murderous music, they trade in blood.

—The New York Times, August 27, 1993

"The **white community doesn't need my money**—they have enough money. The black community needs my money. They need for me to shop in black neighborhoods, stay where I'm needed, stay put. That's where I grew up, so why should I run as soon as I get some money? **Just think: if all the athletes and entertainers stayed in the communities they grew up in, things wouldn't be as bad as they are now."**

—Ice Cube

Reality is in right now in West Coast rap, with Eazy-E, N.W.A and Ice-T leading the way. That means a stark, no-nonsense portrait of ghetto life, where gangs and dope pushers rule.

—Los Angeles Times, April 2, 1989

"**REAL IS AN ART.** Real doesn't necessarily sell. Sometimes it sells. Sometimes it doesn't. The only way you can really be real is not to equate your art with your financial success."

—KRS-One

"Rappers say, "Keep it real and stay hard," yet they're doing fuckin' commercials for potato chips."

—Chubb Rock ▶

"What I try to do is just capture certain moments that stick in my head, certain moments that need to stick in brothers' heads. So it's a little of hip-hop history."

—Rakim

"It's just all a part of being honest about what I'm doing. Whether I'm performing or I'm writing a lyric. I just do it with my sincerest, best foot forward. It's just me being the Busta Rhymes that I am."

—Busta Rhymes

"The definition of a sell-out is someone who comes in hardcore with a street feel and sells to a black audience, but once they start to sell, they leave that audience flat. Someone who is a pop act from the start is not a crossover, because they were never hip-hop to begin with. A lot of hardcore hip-hop acts never get a chance."

—Parrish Smith, EpMd

"This is our art, this is somethin' we worked hard for. We don't really care what any of the media says about it. We're just gonna come out bangin' like we did in '91. We're not supermen. We won't say, 'oh we're the super-gangsters. You can't do shit to me.' Fuck that! In songs I've written, I've actually told people I've been shot. And I have. I still have dreams of being shot that day. You put out what you feel, and people respect the truth."

—B. Real, Cypress Hill

"I don't think that I'm exploiting myself. I talk about where I've been and what I know. A lot of the relation-ships I talk about are a power struggle. I did what I had to do in order to survive, both in relation-ships with guys and just living through major problems in my life. People are definitely misunder-standing me, they're making me out to be a whore and it's not like that. After a woman has been hurt so many times she gets a little hardened, and that's the way I may be. I don't care anymore. People need to stop mis-judging me. 'Cause they really don't know me. It's not like I'm doing it to offend anyone, and pardon me if I did. But my album is something people should listen to in order to understand what is going on. . . . I'm not trying to make a statement."

—Lil' Kim

"I have to make what feels right to me. I can't go out and jump on everybody else's jimmy just to sell records. If my success comes slow, fine, but it'll come."

—Queen Latifah

When he was gunned down in Las Vegas, the rap star Tupac Shakur was under contract to Death Row Records, the West Coast juggernaut that pioneered gangster rap, a wildly successful music made up of misogyny, hypermaterialism and open celebration of murder....The rappers insist they are merely telling it like it is and 'reporting' the news from the ghetto streets. Maybe so. But they were also making a billion-dollar industry into an apparatus for a gang war. The transformation is unprecedented in pop culture; historians will be writing about it for a long time to come. As has been widely reported, Death Row's chief executive, Marion (Suge) Knight, cultivates the gangster image, flaunting the symbols and colors of a Los Angeles street gang. Mr. Knight is the architect of a feud between Death Row in the West and its East Coast rival, Bad Boy Entertainment. The hostilities have been chronicled in trade journals for more than a year and have involved threats, guns and both songs and videos in which rappers insult rivals and depict them coming to harm. Stars who once lived carefree lives now travel with fleets of bodyguards. It is unclear why Mr. Shakur was sprayed with bullets in Las Vegas. But he was the second Death Row insider to be murdered in the last year. The other was Jake Robles, a close friend of Mr. Knight. Mr. Knight was present at both shootings.

—Brent Staples, *The New York Times*, September 22, 1996

"I think the media started the east coast/west coast thing and we fed into it. I think we need to cut that out because we're letting them separate us again. Every time somebody does something for unity, they separate us. So I think that we need to represent hip-hop. That's what we're here for. If you wanna battle, cool, but let's be one generation, not separating rap. And then rap is gonna start fragmenting because it comes from different environments. West coast they talk about lumberjack jackets and 6-4s. Over here we talk about subways. So it's always gonna sound different but we don't have to go at it like it's two different worlds."

—Rakim

"New York is not as important to L.A. We used to want them to accept our music, but now we couldn't care less. I don't mean to dis New York, but I'm tired of them talking all this L.A. crap."

—Tōn-Løc

"Tōn-Løc talks about sex, N.W.A talks about violence. That's why all that stuff sells. A wider audience accepts that kind of shit."

—Afrika Baby-Bam, the Jungle Brothers

"In New York, rap is more political. Poetically, they're very good and God love them for it. But if I want an education, I'll go to school. I think of music as entertainment."

—Matt Dike, producer of Tōn-Lọc and Young MC, co-owner of Delicious Vinyl records

"In New York, they've already been through all the gang stuff, all the bragging about cars, girls, and gold. Now, there's a cultural awareness that's happening in the East, and it's stretching across the country. It's just taking a longer time for L.A. to become aware."

—Afrika Bambaataa

"Rap is rebellious music and we have a hard enough time being accepted. Competing against each other ain't making things no better. When all the dissin' stops, we'll all achieve more success. Unfortunately, there are still a few ignorant brothers out there who work on that level."

—Big Daddy Kane

"You don't see R&B or rock groups attacking each other all the time. **A rivalry between New York and L.A. is senseless.**"

—Eric B.

"I admit New York is proud of its own. But now it doesn't matter where your records come from. West coast, east coast, north, south, overseas. If a record sounds good, I'm playing it."

—Kool DJ Red Alert

ICE CUBE ▶

Suge Knight rolled into the music industry, a 315-pound banquet cart of scandal who had eight criminal convictions and five contracts on his life in the six years he was an executive before being imprisoned for parole violations last year. The gangsta-rap label he ran, Death Row (once home to Tupac Shakur, Snoop Doggy Dogg and Dr. Dre), upped the ante of music-industry corruption from a sleazy world of payola and sexual harassment to a dangerous battleground where enemies were pistol-whipped or mysteriously disappeared, the label's own artists were beaten at company meetings and contract negotiations were made with baseball bats instead of pens. Equal parts *The Godfather*, *Scarface*, *The Mack* and *Colors*, the rise and fall of Death Row is, along with the suicide of Kurt Cobain, one of the most important and tragic stories of pop music in the 90s, culminating in the drive-by shootings of two top rappers, Shakur and the Notorious B.I.G.

—Neil Strauss, *The New York Times*, March 3, 1998

"Suge Knight is really, really talented. He has operated from the beginning on a lot of gut instinct. And over a short period of time he's developed his own frame of reference, he understands the industry now, and he's proving himself every day. I've seen him grow so much over such a short period of time, he's grown as big and as fast as his records."

—Russell Simmons

"Chuck isn't too much of a joker, but Flav will drive you up a wall. Like Raid to the roaches."

—Flavor Flav ▶

"When we went on our first tour people couldn't really separate the lyrics from us. They thought that was what we were, which always seemed weird, because a lot of the stuff on the first album was just us having a good time and coming up with stories. Like, Adam [Horovitz] would be rockin' the lederhosen, and people in England would be like, Is this a serious thing? And we'd be like, Not really."

—Mike D., the Beastie Boys

"Controversy and gangster stuff attracts all the writers, and that gets them to write about basically nothing. There's no substance in the records, no substance in the vinyl. Most of these guys making these gangster records are not even tough enough to baby-sit."

—Chubb Rock

"Everything we say already exists. 'Fuck tha Police' and 'Don't Believe the Hype' have been around for a long time; people just said, 'Oh, fuck the police,' or, 'The media is bullshit.'"

—KRS-One

109

"The first gig we ever played as Eric B. and Rakim was Latin Quarter. I thought it was going to be rough up there. I had no stage moves. I just held the mic and spit into it. I didn't jump around, didn't dance. People were coming out with dances and gimmicks, I just came out, grabbed the mic, spit my shit, and I was like yo, boom, boom, boom. It was butterflies before that, but once the crowd opened their arms, it was O.K. and I blessed 'em."

—Rakim

MOST OF MY HEROES DON'T APPEAR ON NO STAMPS

After two and a half centuries of slavery, followed by a century of rural semi-serfdom and violently imposed segregation, wanton economic discrimination, and outright exclusion of Afro-Americans from the middle and upper echelons of the nation's economy, it was inevitable that when the nation finally committed itself to the goal of ethnic justice and integration the transition would be painful, if not traumatic. The prejudices of centuries die hard, and even when they wane, the institutional frameworks that sustained them are bound to linger. . . . The enormity of the achievement of the last forty years in American ethnic relations cannot be overstated. For better or worse, the Afro-American presence in American life and thought is today pervasive. A mere 13 percent of the population, Afro-Americans dominate the nation's popular culture: its music, its dance, its talk, its sports, its youth fashion; and they are a powerful force in its popular and elite literatures. So powerful and unavoidable is the Afro-American popular influence that it is now common to find people who, while remaining racists in personal relations and attitudes, nonetheless have surrendered their tastes, and much of their viewing and listening time, to Afro-American entertainers, talk-show hosts, and sitcom stars. . . the typical rap fan is an upper-middle-class, Euro-American suburban youth.

—Orlando Patterson, *The Paradoxes of Integration*

"**The original man started going against his nature by telling lies, stealing, and using trick knowledge** and that same person was named **YAKUB—'JACOB'** in the Bible. Within the black man there is a black germ and a brown germ, and the brown germ is the weak germ. As you graft it, you go from black to brown, from brown to red, from red to yellow, and from yellow to white. And white is the final weakness."

—Lord Jamar, Brand Nubian

113

"**Brothers and sisters are typecast** like we're from some other fuckin' **planet**, which is made out of **concrete**."

—Chuck D

"A lot of white kids buy rap, because they're finally trying to learn about what we're doing, just like they did rock 'n' roll. They're trying to understand where some of this shit is coming from. 'Cause even some of the white kids go through the same shit in their neighborhoods. They may have money, but **a lot of rich kids are sick in the fucking head.** A lot of kids in the suburbs go through problems. Everybody has problems, and I think that's why some of these kids are relating to the hardcore shit these days."

—B. Real, Cypress Hill

"You're not gonna see many white people doing rap because **THE MAJORITY OF WHITE PEOPLE DO NOT HAVE RHYTHM.** Because they don't grow up in the streets. **Rap music is from the streets.** Blacks created rap music but others can play it. I rap straight from the heart. I write my own lyrics. A lot of people don't want to give me respect, 'cause my music is on the pop side and I'm white. I've been doing this for years, man. I'm expressing myself through rap music no matter what color I am. Rap music is all about expression anyway. I'm not a white guy trying to be black. **Nobody wants to give me credit because I'm white. I've been called white nigger,** I've been called wannabe black. I've been called all kinds of things. People can't accept that a white kid did grow up in the streets."

—Vanilla Ice

◀ **CYPRESS HILL**

▲ HOUSE OF PAIN
◄ EVERLAST

"Pop culture is a melting pot, so when we talk about urban music, we don't exclude anybody. Most of what we do is founded on black experience, but also in how people receive the information from African America. We're challenging people's assumptions about culture and music, about who should be doing what, about black and white, about what these terms mean. How can you define anybody with colors from a Crayola pack? We're talking about culture."

—Bill Stephney, producer

"Some say this country will never stop being racist. Well, that doesn't mean you throw up your hands. You acquire your own power, taking away other people's power over you. That's just taking back what should have been yours anyway."

—Spike Lee

"Elektra is a white company, but if we can use it to get our message across to the youth, to the babies, to all original people—original people meaning the black man, the first man—then we gotta take that step. And if it means putting out records for a white company, then that's a small sacrifice."

—Sadat X, Brand Nubian

"Our song 'Gas Face' definitely would have sold a lot more and gotten more play on MTV if we had left out lyrics like, 'must have been a white guy who started all that,' but **we don't hide from the white-black issue** and the problems it creates in the record industry."

—Pete Nice, 3rd Bass

"Picture a white, liberal family—racist—traditional American family. They're scared to death because their son is in his room listening to N.W.A and Public Enemy and the kid is growing up on that."

—2 Black 2 Strong

"All these white kids wanna be black now.
All these white boys—baseball caps, fuckin' pants
saggin'. The scary part is, they're really in tune
now, really holdin' 40s. They're playin' a game they
don't understand."

—Erick Sermon, EpMd

"I know white people, like
schoolteachers I had,
that I loved. Loved 'em! And
there's some black friends that
I have that's the worst people
in the world. So who's
my devil that I gotta
look out for?"

—Rakim

"**The darker your skin is, the stronger you are.** Just look at the universe. When the sun comes down, white people get tan and the body has to produce more melanin to protect itself. **But** there is only so much melanin that the body can produce before you start burning up. **And whether they tell you or not, melanin has to do with mentality.** Anything physical is reflective of the mental. And the dark-skinned man has nothing to worry about with the sun. If you have a large amount of melanin the sun gives you energy. If you're gonna say, The darker you are, the better you are, that's true. The darker your mind is, the blacker your mind is, the better off you are. **I mean, when you close your eyes, what do you see? You don't see white, you see black.**"

—Lord Jamar, Brand Nubian

121

"Racism is one of those things where, if you're a mathematician and the teacher says, 'I want you to calculate to the last digit the sum of pi,' you say, 'I don't know the answer yet, but I'm gonna keep working.' And the teacher sees you getting frustrated and says, 'There is no answer—it's gonna go on forever.' That's how I see racism. **YOU'RE MADE TO BELIEVE THAT THERE IS NO ANSWER TO RACISM, THAT YOU WAKE UP BORN A RACIST AND THAT'S IT.** To me, I feel there is an answer. I sat down and watched Geraldo when he had **KKK** members on there and a woman with her little baby in a hood. And I don't feel hatred for them. They just don't know."

—**Chubb Rock** ▸

"I just got back from a little resort. I had three days off, and I was the only black one there. **Who was running the kitchens, who was sweeping the floor, who was vacuuming the pool? All black.** And I'm in there feeling uncomfortable. And I'm leaning over the pool, giving my man a hand, like 'Yo, what up?' **The only people who will talk to me are the maintenance people.** Those are the only ones I can relate to."

—**Parrish Smith, EpMd**

CASH
MOVES EVERYTHING
AROUND ME

A little over 29 percent of all Afro-American persons—
some 9,873,000 souls—and slightly over a quarter of all Afro-
American families (26.4 percent) were poor as of March 1996.
Afro-American individuals are 2.6 times more likely to be poor
than Euro-Americans, and their families are slightly more than
three times more vulnerable to poverty.

In 1995, a total of 4,552,000 Afro-American children, com-
prising 41.5 percent of Afro-American children under age 18
living in families, were poor.

—Orlando Patterson, *The Paradoxes of Integration*

"This is a **demoralizing business.**
People will do **anything** for money. There is
no limit to what they'll do. They'll sell **drugs,**
sell **ass,** sell **records,** sell **bricks,** you
know what I'm sayin'? But if there is an influx
and everyone's saying '**suck my dick**'
and those are the number one records, Ali,
Phife, and Tip are not going to be making
records that say, 'suck my dick,' all the time."

—Q-Tip, A Tribe Called Quest

"What **bugged me out** is that the first check I got was for **$17,000.** That's when I said, O.K., this shit is kinda crazy. I think it was because I had a lot of attention when I was younger that it didn't blow my head up. I was still doing the same things. People wanted to know why I didn't leave the neighborhood. Then when I did leave the neighborhood, people want to know why I didn't stay. **I learned you couldn't please everybody."**

—Rakim

"A lot of people think I'm something that I know I'm not. I'm not saying I don't want to be a Berry Gordy in the future, I'm young and I'm gonna be around for a long time, but there's a little stress right now to prove myself. It feels good though, better to have this type of stress than be in O.J. Simpson's category. Know what I'm sayin'?"

—Puff Daddy

"They used to call brothers that 'make it' token blacks, 'cause the whole neighborhood's still smokin' crack. If your brothers ain't made it, you ain't made it. If I don't give what I got, somebody's gonna take it."

—Ice Cube

129

◄ ICE-T (FRONT) & ICE CUBE

"I'm not doing this to get paid. I've always loved to do this because I appreciate the **art form.** I really like this. And I could do other things— I'm alright. **I'm not in it for this money."**

—L.L. Cool J ▸

"My mother and father hated rap. They'd say, Why are you wasting your time? My God! Your whole life. Then as soon as they found out I was serious about it and got a deal they're saying, Oh rap—boy, rap sounds beautiful don't it?"

—Shazzy

"Any time anybody stays satisfied with what they have, they start slippin'. So we stayed hungry. Stayed in our neighborhoods, and we didn't let the success with the record business go to our heads. It's a little easier, making money legally, but basically, we still go through the same shit. Money can't fix everything. So we just put our frustrations into the music."

—B. Real, Cypress Hill

"Rap is out of control. Before, there was such a thing as a crossover. NOW THE UNDER-GROUND IS THE MAINSTREAM. People are motivated by greed and they're headed toward a false picture they know nothing about."

—Parrish Smith, EpMd

"The more you have access to the media, the more opportunity you have to speak out. Luke Perry was on a magazine cover posing with a gun. But his world consists of sunshine, L.A. women, and the whole nine. Our world consists of underground, strictly funk street attitude. The magazines are gonna do what they wanna do. But there's no longevity in controversy. Anyway, we don't feel our whole career should be based on the media."

—Parrish Smith, EpMd

133

"A problem in the rap fanzines is that they check every artist for blackness. If you aren't wearing a dashiki, you're not legitimate to them. If Quincy Jones and Warner do something, it might be more straight up—stick to the music. If Hammer has 15 million fans and you ignore him, you're ignoring 15 million people, which doesn't make much sense. Maybe I should start my own magazine."

—Sir Mix-A-Lot

"In my early years I read *Rap Masters, Word Up!, Right On!*, and *Black Beat*, all for their so-called **black agenda.** As I became more experienced, I realized that this black agenda is **paid for by white advertisers** looking to reach the black consumer. I personally have not yet found a total hip-hop magazine, because for one thing, you must understand black people to understand rap. Second thing, **a total hip-hop magazine is bound to offend advertisers.** If you know that Chuck D. has a whole crusade against malt liquor being targeted to the black community, why would you, as a hip-hop magazine, accept alcohol advertising dollars and promote alcohol?"

—KRS-One

"Now with the growth in rap media, things are more likely to be misunderstood and lead to controversy. But the plus outweighs the minus. Anything that can show the different aspects of rappers and hip-hop is good. But it's definitely dangerous new territory."

—Chubb Rock

"When I see Demi Moore on the cover of *Vanity Fair* in her birthday suit, the painted-on suit, I know I could never do that. If it was Queen Latifah, or any other female rapper, it would be like 'Oh, my God, what are these rappers doing now, telling our children to go out and pose nude?' I want to see magazines report, but I just hope they don't try to change rap into something it's not and end up fuckin' up the whole art form."

—Michelle, Bytches with Problems

BY ANY MEANS
NECESSARY

"You have to make a lot of sacrifices. You can't even pose before yourself the alternative of, What am I going to do? Am I going to stay home and get high and have a good time tonight, or am I going to go out to try and rap with the people, to try to organize? You don't have that alternative anymore. I have given my life to the struggle."

—Angela Y. Davis

"Yo. We ain't campaigning. We're here to tell the truth. We're not politicians."

—Wise Intelligent,
Poor Righteous Teachers

"We're not a political act, so we don't try to beat anybody over the head with how we feel about certain things. We like to put out slammin' and dope tracks. We touch upon different subjects and then we move on."

—Phife, A Tribe Called Quest

"THERE'S A REASON WHY RAPPERS HAVE BEEN PLACED IN THE POSITION OF BEING SORTA LIKE THE NEW BLACK LEADERSHIP IN THIS COUNTRY FOR YOUNG PEOPLE. In the 1960s and 1970s there was an effort by the CIA and Co Intellpro to either execute or incarcerate or force into exile all of the black leadership. And that made it very easy for the Reagan-Bush administration to cut 40 billion dollars in social spending. Mostly from the black community without any black leadership to cry out. So in the late 1980s, you see a lot of young people using rap to attack government policies. **The problem is that many of these rappers aren't completely informed. So they're attacking symbols of authority rather than direct authority.** So on one hand, it's good that rap music has given a voice for young people to express things politically. On the other hand, **some of the people who have been elevated to a leadership status because of the vacuum of black leadership haven't been totally with it as far as their under-standing of what is going on in the world, and that is where you get this hypocrisy."**

—Michael Franti, *Disposable Heroes of Hiphoprisy*

139

"I'm not on a **political mission**. I'm not gonna go around **kissing babies,** answering questions ambiguously, and frontin' because I want people to love me."

—L.L. Cool J

"Carter was the one President who felt a little funny about killing people. When you're **George Bush**, you really don't give a shit. He's got mad dough, a gold chain, and a beeper the size of the world. Holding his dick, saying, '**Fuck all of y'all.**'"

—KRS-One

"Why is it only at election time that politicians go into the black community? What are they gonna do? In a land where we have nothing, come in and promise us the world?"

—Parrish Smith, EpMd

141

"It can be called black nationalism, it might be called separatism, it might be called racist. But all we are saying is it is time for us to clean up our home. If someone considers it racism or separatism, there's nothing I can do about it. All I know is we want to bring young people to this state of mind, see that we are in control of our destiny."

—Professor X

"I know that **societies** often have killed the people who have helped to **change** those societies. And if I can die having brought any light, having exposed any meaningful truth that will help to destroy the **racist cancer** that is malignant in the body of America—then all of the credit is due to Allah. **Only the mistakes have been mine.**"

—Malcolm X,
The Autobiography of Malcolm X

ABOUT THE AUTHORS

Gregor Ehrlich is a writer living in New York City, whose work has appeared in *Spin, Might, Hits, Pulse, New York, Interview* and other publications.

Dimitri Ehrlich has written for *The New York Times, Rolling Stone, Spin, Details, Vibe, Entertainment Weekly,* and *Interview Magazine,* where he is a contributing editor. He is the author of *Inside the Music: Conversations with Contemporary Musicians about Spirituality, Creativity, and Consciousness* (Shambhala Publications). He is also a musician whose most recent album, *As Nervous As You* (Tainted Records), has no rapping on it whatsoever.

```
782.4216 Ehrlich, Gregor.
49
Ehr        Move the crowd.
```

DATE			
25 July 06			